A PLUME BOOK

I'D RATHER BE SHORT

Half Orange Photography

BECKY MURPHY is a freelance designer and illustrator based out of Austin, Texas. She grew up in small-town Iowa, honed her craft at Iowa State, then, like a bird, moved south. Becky will high-five if provoked, but don't make her jump to reach it. You can see more of her work on her site, chipperthings.com.

I'd Rather Be SHORT

100 Reasons why it's GREAT to be Small

Becky Murphy

A PLUME BOOK

PLUME
Published by the Penguin Group
Penguin Group (USA) LLC
375 Hudson Street,
New York, New York 10014

USA | Canada | UK | Ireland | Australia | New Zealand | India | South Africa | China
penguin.com
A Penguin Random House Company

First published by Plume, a member of Penguin Group (USA) LLC, 2013

 REGISTERED TRADEMARK—MARCA REGISTRADA

ISBN 978-0-14-219698-4

Printed in the United States of America
10 9 8 7 6 5 4 3 2 1

Set in Interstate

For you!
(and my mom and dad)

INTRODUCTION

Hello, short friend.

I'm glad we found each other. Welcome to the biggest little hall of fame list. I'm assuming you didn't pick up this book because of your fixation with crossword puzzles or because you were hoping to breeze through a pictorial biography of Queen Elizabeth. I'm guessing it had something to do with the title coinciding with you being particularly small in stature. You've come to the right place.

If you had to climb the shelf to reach this book, I understand your plight—I'm five feet tall (on a good day). My hair has 5'5" potential and sometimes I wear shoes that make me look like an anime character (platforms, guys). Being the same size as a fifth grader is often fantastic; I can fit in their cheap clothes, yet I'm old enough to drive myself to interesting places like, say, the office. Nobody expects me to clean the fan blades or replace the water cooler, and I can maneuver to the front of the crowd during concerts. But, to be honest, I didn't always like being short. I knew there was nothing wrong with it, but I felt conspicuous when strangers would point out my height before even learning my name. (I'm glad they got the burden off their chests right away. What if I didn't know?! What if I was gallivanting about as if I was a . . . a . . . Leggy Laura?) Well, I'm here to say thank you, strangers along the way, for you have empowered me to chronicle our points of pride. If morose dinosaurs and unicorn jerks get their own books, then shorties of the world should get one, too.

I'd Rather Be Short is exactly what it sounds like—a declaration of pride in who we are. This little (zing!) collection contains the obvious (you're always the limbo champ!) and the subtle (you're less intimidating) reasons to celebrate being short. You've probably already noticed that you're the master of chicken fights and that you've never had to duck for shower heads, but did you know that 80 percent of your mischief goes unnoticed by law-abiding citizens? (Unconfirmed.) Maybe you've never noticed the advantages of your height because you haven't known life any other way. It doesn't matter. What does matter is that you recognize this: Short is good, and there are at least as many reasons in this book as there are counties in Iowa to prove it.

This book was written under the umbrella of self-acceptance. The sooner we are okay with being different from one another, the sooner we can get on with being the best version of ourselves and love how we were created. These sometimes-awkward, sometimes-savvy illustrations have found their way to your eyeballs, and I hope they settle into your heart, too. (If the Mother Teresa page doesn't do it for you, then try the one with Shakespeare. After that, I can't help you.)

If your self-esteem isn't already as big as Machu Picchu, it will be after you read this book. If nothing else, you'll finally have a handy list of retaliations the next time an average-size bystander says, "You're so small I could just put you in my pocket!" or "I'm going to call you Pocket [name]!" or "You make even me feel tall!" or "I should totally use you as an armrest!" Those clever beanpoles have no idea what's coming.

Short friends, we need to be here for one another. And that starts with buying several copies of this book. I'm talking, like, so many copies. Purchase one for yourself and for every one of your short friends. My publisher also suggests keeping one in your glove compartment as a spare.

If nothing else, let's band together under this common goal: Let us make shortness so accepted, so popular, so desirable, that one day, aliens will look at our civilization and say, "How did the short people get away with so much braggery? This is worse than the grandma wallets we found in Reno."

Forever short (not only because I have to be, but proud that I get to be),

1. You can sleep like a queen in a twin-size bed.

2. No heels are too high. Go gangbusters.

3. You can't outgrow tree houses.

4. Kids' clothes: expanding options while saving money.

5. You get thrown around . . . ON THE DANCE FLOOR.

6. You're more unique—like diamonds, albinos,
or limited edition Beanie Babies.

7. You are amazing at the limbo.

8. You're less likely to smell people's bad breath.

9. Your face never gets cut off in group photos—because
you're always in the front.

10. You never have to carry the umbrella.

11. You're never expected to help your friends move. (Unless you have a truck, or a heart the size of Texas.)

12. You're an easy overnight guest. You love
love seats and they love you.

13. 50 Cent wants to party in the club with you.
Like it's your *birthday* or something.

14. If you have a firm handshake, it surprises people.
Then they decide you must be a real go-getter.

15. You get to sit on laps rather than being sat on.

16. You're less likely to get hit by a bullet.

17. You can easily turn a pillowcase into a costume.

18. Short shorts can be appropriate for you anytime, anywhere.

19. You get your friends' shrunken clothes.

20. You never have a double chin from anyone else's perspective.

Jockey

Libero

Flyer

Coxswain

IA - 319

Olympic Gymnast

21. You excel in a number of sports thanks to your height.

22. Thanks to your hair to height ratio, you can have mermaid hair in no time.

23. You'll be super cute when you're old.

24. You're less intimidating . . . when you want to be.

25. The shorter you are, the softer the fall.

26. You're never the one to make the hot tub overflow.

27. Your size is conducive to chair-sharing.

28. You are automatically awesome at hide-and-seek.

29. You're more likely to get a piggyback ride home when you're really tired.

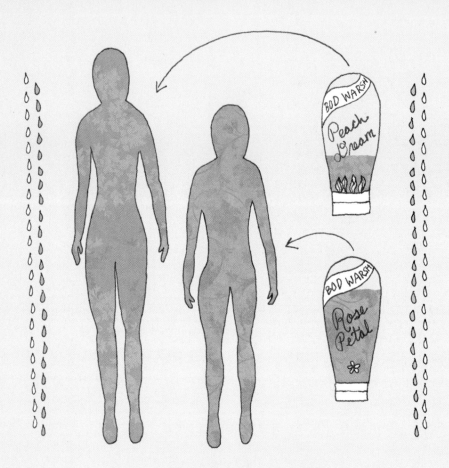

30. You save money on body wash.

31. You are a fantastic candidate for a fantastic hug.

32. Tall chores just aren't expected of you.

33. You have a smaller strike zone.

34. You're always the one who gets hoisted into attics, trees, and windows by your taller friends.

35. Because you're less threatening, you never have to defend
yourself against animals.

36. You're always a "step up."

37. Kiddie pools were made for you.

38. You join the likes of respectable ladies such as Amy Poehler, Dolly Parton, Natalie Portman, and Salma Hayek.

39. You get the best of both worlds: kids' meals and cocktail parties.

40. You don't have to duck for branches when ambling through the forest on your pony.

41. You make your significant other feel significantly taller than they actually are.

42. You're harder to take down in a chicken fight.

43. Fake studies show that the smaller you are, the less likely
you are to get a speeding ticket.

44. You can say you can't fight the heavyweight champion
because of "reach."

45. It takes less time to shave your legs.

46. It's easier to escape through non-egress windows during a fire or bear attack.

47. A lower center of gravity makes for better balance.

48. Skirts can be dresses and dresses can be skirts.

49. It's easier to blend into crowds when an enemy is chasing you.

50. You can stand in an airplane under the storage units,
and you don't even have to slouch.

51. Food portions seem bigger.

52. It cannot be stressed enough how valuable it is to be able to fit into small spaces.

53. Concertgoers are less likely to hassle you when you shimmy
up to the front.

54. You're always the little spoon. No-brainer.

55. A laundry basket could be a sled for you.

56. It's cheaper and faster to make your own clothes.

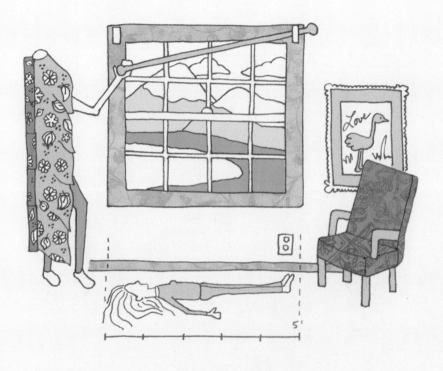

57. Short people make excellent measuring sticks, particularly for
rearranging living room furniture.

58. *This* still happens.

59. Sample shoes at department stores fit you.

60. You're generally more space-efficient.

61. Since people assume you don't need "that much," they are
quick to share with you.

62. County fair: short people can get in for free and *still* make it into the beer tent.

63. Short people have faster reaction times.

64. You can scale shelves like a pro.

65. You're less likely to get struck by lightning.

66. If you can dunk, you become an instant hero like
Spud Webb or Teen Wolf.

67. Short women are adorable when they're pregnant.
Good luck finding someone who disagrees.

68. It's easier to get pants hemmed than it is to magically make them grow.

69. You're more likely to lose cannonball contests, but it's okay because having the smallest splash is what really makes you a winner.

70. Every seat in the car has ample leg room.

71. You're scrappier.

72. You never have to duck for showerheads.

73. You can drink at your own pace because nobody
expects you to keep up.

74. Big hair is extra big. Perfect for living in the South or going to Amy Winehouse tribute parties.

75. You have stronger muscles in proportion to your weight.

76. You can curl up like a cat and sleep on a plane.

77. Nobody ever thinks the small one is guilty.

78. Being short lends itself to classic pickup lines: "I can't reach that toilet paper . . . BUTT I bet you can."

79. Tall people are jealous of you because while they can't shrink, you can still "grow."

80. You can jump on beds without hitting your head on the ceiling.

81. Smaller clothes = more space for souvenirs.

82. Shaq-size playground equipment just doesn't exist.

83. You have the ability to sit cross-legged *anywhere*.

84. Since sizes from the olden days ran much smaller, your vintage finds increase tenfold.

85. You impress people when you carry heavy objects. Bonus points when said objects are bigger than you.

86. You're easier to protect.

87. You have an array of nicknames that either start with "Lil" or end in "Smalls."

88. You can easily find "luxury" apartments when all ceilings
are high ceilings.

89. You don't have to stand up when people walk to their seats
in the movie theater.

90. You look cuter and crazier when flailing your arms on
the dance floor.

91. You see the world from a different perspective . . . just like
Mother Teresa did.

"Though she be but little, she is fierce!"
—Bill

92. Shakespeare fancies your petite stature.

93. Tall friends are like free bodyguards.

94. You can catapult yourself onto others with the guarantee you cannot crush them.

Fencing Team Captain
Drama Club President
Student Council President
Yearbook editor-in-chief
Debate Team Captain
Beekeepers President
Wrestling Manager
Class Secretary
Wildcat Mascot

95. Being short probably builds character.

96. Hotel towels actually fit you.

97. It's easier to hold hands with a child.

98. Your youthful glow will never fade.

99. They say if you're short, you can pull off anything.

100. You're just the way you should be.

ACKNOWLEDGMENTS

*I*f you are actually reading the acknowledgments page, you either really liked the book or you hope to find yourself listed below. Either way, this page is for you.

It's not fair that my name is the only one on the cover because it wouldn't exist if it weren't for my supportive community. I didn't give myself these hands, but I'm grateful I have them to illustrate with.

Mom and Dad get the biggest slice of the thank-you pie. You two have encouraged, nudged, expected, dreamed, and celebrated all of my artistic endeavors. Dad knows perseverance like Mom knows art.

Thank you, Ryan, Candice, Brock, and Laurel for not being surprised when I told you that this idea just might work. Huge thanks to Chad Conine for getting me started, copious amounts of edits, and encouragement from day one; Amy Butler for that Shmaltz's pep talk (and many since); Bekah Brown for doing the tall chores and being such a supportive friend; Matthew Genitempo and Jonathan Standefer for teaching me how to use the Internet; Andy Keil for forcing me to hurry up and follow my dreams; Beth Nervig for doing edits on demand; my life group, who experienced the highs and lows week after week and still managed to celebrate with me; Hole in the Roof for the incredible support; Grace and Karol Ladd for your uplifting words and wisdom; Madison, Alicia, Caitlin, Hannah, and everyone else who still called me during the months of book hibernation.

Shout-out to hot tea, computers, V5 pens, watercolor paper, Photoshop, Gmail, documentaries, chairs, and ice cream. I couldn't have done it without you either.

Huge hugs and high-fives for Laurie Abkemeier, the greatest agent in all the land. Thank you for representing me with such a silly project; I couldn't have asked for anyone better to work with. Thanks to my editor, Kate Napolitano, for putting your heart into each round of edits and dealing with my long-winded e-mails. I never dreamed that my agent and editor would give me so much creative freedom.

Thank you Iowa friends, Waco and Austin friends, family members, Twitter followers, and blog readers. My dream could not have come true if it weren't for your help, whether it be big or small (last short pun).

I am eternally grateful.